Pushing 40

Other For Better or For Worse® Books

It's All Downhill From Here
Keep the Home Fries Burning
Just One More Hug
It Must Be Nice to Be Little
Is This "One of Those Days," Daddy?
I've Got the One-More-Washload Blues

Pushing 40

A *For Better or For Worse* Collection
by Lynn Johnston

Andrews and McMeel
A Universal Press Syndicate Company
Kansas City • New York

ISBN: 0-8362-1807-8
Library of Congress Catalog Card Number: 88-71103

First Printing, July 1988
Third Printing, December 1988

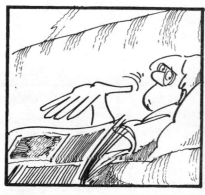

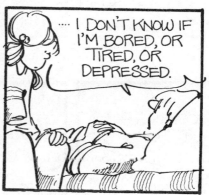

I GET SO TIRED OF THE CONSTANT BICKERING, CONNIE. WHY CAN'T MY TWO KIDS JUST TRY TO GET ALONG?!

I SUPPOSE YOU AND YOUR BROTHER NEVER FOUGHT.

OF COURSE WE DID!

BUT ONE DAY WE REALIZED THAT WE REALLY LOVED EACH OTHER, AND WE COULD ACCOMPLISH MORE AS FRIENDS THAN ENEMIES.

UNFORTUNATELY, WE WERE BOTH IN OUR TWENTIES AT THE TIME.

ELIZABETH! BEDTIME! IT'S BEDTIME, HONEY.

ELIZABETH? ELIZABETH, IT'S TIME TO COME IN!

ELIZABETH, YOU GET IN THE HOUSE THIS MINUTE — OR ELSE!!!

... I LIKE TO WAIT 'TIL SHE MEANS IT!

SHE'S, SHE'S TURNING AROUND! SHE'S STRETCHING!

OH, WOW! NOW SHE'S COMING OVER TO THE WINDOW!

THAT'S FUNNY...

THERE'S NO WIND TONIGHT, BUT THAT WHOLE TREE OVER THERE SEEMS TO BE MOVING!!

THIS IS A TRULY INCREDIBLE NIGHT, GUYS...

OH, NO! SHE'S CLOSED THE CURTAINS! SHE'S CLOSED THE STUPID CURTAINS!!!

WHAT'S THE MATTER? IT'S NOT MY FAULT! WHY ARE YOU ALL LOOKING AT ME?!!

IT'S YOUR TREE.

MAN, I'VE NEVER SPIED IN A GIRL'S BEDROOM BEFORE!

COME ON! LET'S GET OUTA HERE BEFORE SOMEBODY SEES US!!

GUYS... DO ANY OF YOU KNOW THE LORD'S PRAYER?

OK, OK, THIS IS THE PLAN...

SHE CAN'T CATCH ALL OF US—SO EVERYBODY JUMP DOWN AT THE SAME TIME AN' RUN IN DIFFERENT DIRECTIONS!

I DON'T WANT EVERY-BODY, PATTERSON!

JUST YOU!!!

OH, MAN—SHE'S GOT MICHAEL! SHE'S GOT 'IM BY THE NECK!

I WISH WE HADN'T BEEN SPYING IN HER WINDOW. WE'RE IN BIG TROUBLE NOW!

I'LL PROBABLY GET GROUNDED!

I'LL LOSE MY ALLOWANCE FOR A MONTH!

IT WOULD ALL BE WORTH IT, GUYS... IF ONLY WE'D SEEN SOMETHING!!!

HONEST, MOLLY—WE DIDN'T...

CAN IT, PATTERSON.

MAN, IF I EVER CATCH YOU EVEN THINKING OF SPYING ON ME AGAIN, KNOW WHAT I'M GONNA DO?

I'LL TELL THE COPS! I'LL TELL YOUR PRINCIPAL! I'LL TELL EVERY KID YOU KNOW THAT YOU'RE A PERVERT! UNDER-STAND?

UH HUH.

PLEASE! JUST DON'T TELL MY DAD!!

YOU? SPYING IN A GIRL'S WINDOW? MIKE! THIS IS SERIOUS!

I COULDN'T HELP IT! WE WERE IN THE TREE, AN' THE WINDOW WAS THERE AN'....

BUT WE DIDN'T SEE ANYTHING, DAD! ....UH, DAD? WHAT'RE YOU GONNA DO TO ME?

THE SAME THING MY DAD DID TO ME THE DAY I PUT A PERISCOPE UP TO THE MOON IN THE DOOR OF KENNEDY'S OUTHOUSE.

AAAAAAGHH!! GROUNDED FOR TWO WEEKS?! I'LL DIE!!

I CAN'T GO OFF THE BLOCK, I HAFTA BE IN OUR YARD BY 4:00 EVERY DAY, AN' I CAN'T GO OUT AFTER SUPPER!

THIS IS TORTURE!! HOW AM I GONNA LIVE THROUGH THIS?!!

THE QUESTION IS.... HOW AM I GONNA LIVE THROUGH THIS?!!

ONE DUMB THING. I DID ONE DUMB THING, AN' NOW I HAFTA SUFFER FOR TWO WHOLE WEEKS!

EVER WISH YOU COULD LIVE A DAY OVER AGAIN, BRIAN? EVER WISH YOU COULD ERASE EVERYTHING AN' START AGAIN?

YEAH.

IF WE COULD RELIVE THE OTHER NIGHT, WE NEVER WOULDA BEEN SPYING IN MOLLY'S ROOM IN THE FIRST PLACE!

IF WE COULD RELIVE THE OTHER NIGHT..... WE NEVER WOULDA BEEN CAUGHT!

STAND STILL, HONEY. I WANT TO GET YOUR DRESS JUST RIGHT.

OH, I'M SO EXCITED, JOHN! THIS IS SUCH A BEAUTIFUL DAY FOR A WEDDING!

LOOK AT THE FLOWER GIRL, MICHAEL. ISN'T ELIZABETH PRETTY?

YEAH!

SHE LOOKS TOO GOOD TO BE MY SISTER!

MIKE! LIZZIE! HURRY UP, OR WE'LL BE LATE FOR PHIL AND GEORGIA'S WEDDING!

HONEY, WHY ARE YOU PUTTING THE GARBAGE INTO THE BACK OF THE CAR?

I THOUGHT WE COULD DROP IT OFF AT THE DUMP ON THE WAY.

GO TO THE DUMP? BUT WHY?!!

JUST THE OTHER DAY YOU SAID I NEVER TAKE YOU ANY- WHERE!

COUGH, COUGH - BLEAH! CAN WE OPEN A WINDOW?

JOHN, I AM NOT GOING TO THE DUMP! YOU CAN TAKE US TO THE CHURCH AND DROP THE GARBAGE OFF LATER!

BUT IT'S JULY! DO YOU KNOW WHAT THE CAR WILL BE LIKE IF WE DON'T GO TO THE DUMP?

PUT IT THIS WAY... DO YOU KNOW WHAT I WILL BE LIKE IF WE DO?!!

15

FRENCH BRAIDS? ELIZABETH LET YOU BRAID HER HAIR?

HOW COME YOU'LL SIT STILL FOR GRANDMA, BUT YOU WON'T SIT STILL FOR ME?

WE GRANDMAS HAVE A SPECIAL WAY WITH LITTLE ONES DON'T WE, ELIZABETH.

UH HUH.

...SHE PAID ME A BUCK!

HOW LONG CAN YOU STAY, GRAMPA?

JUST A FEW DAYS.

I HAVE TO GET BACK FOR A REUNION WITH SOME OF THE CHAPS I KNEW IN THE AIR FORCE.

EVERY YEAR WE LIKE TO GET TOGETHER TO SEE EACH OTHER, TO SEE WHO'S DOING WHAT...

....TO SEE WHO'S STILL THERE.

WHAT'S IT LIKE TO BE OLD, GRAMPA?

OLD? 65 ISN'T OLD!! I'M A YOUNG MAN, MIKE. I'M ACTIVE, INTELLIGENT—I'M IN MY PRIME! 65 IS NOTHING MORE THAN A NUMBER.

'BULGE'

...A ROUNDED FIGURE, AS IT WERE.

LOOK AT THIS, GUYS! I GOT YOU BOTH YOUR SCHOOL SUPPLIES!

NEW SCRIBBLERS, NEW PENCILS, CRAYONS, SCISSORS— EVERYTHING!

OH, I JUST LOVED GETTING THESE THINGS WHEN I WAS YOUR AGE! I LOVED THE LOOK, THE FEEL, THE SMELL...

WANNA SEE IF MOM'S OK, DAD? SHE'S UPSTAIRS SNIFFING ERASERS.

DON'T PUT THAT OUTFIT ON, LIZZIE—IT'S FOR SCHOOL!

OH. WELL, ALL RIGHT— BUT DON'T GO OUTSIDE. JUST WEAR IT IN HERE.

LIZZIE, IF YOU'RE GOING TO WEAR THAT OUTFIT OUTSIDE, YOU'D BETTER NOT GET IT DIRTY!

NEXT YEAR, I BUY THEIR SCHOOL CLOTHES AFTER THEY'VE GONE BACK TO SCHOOL!!

HI, CONNIE! ARE THE GIRLS LOOKING FORWARD TO STARTING IN A NEW SCHOOL?

GAYLE IS. SHE WANTS TO GET BACK INTO BASKETBALL, MEET NEW FRIENDS .... BUT MOLLY IS ANOTHER STORY.

SHE'S SPENT THE WHOLE SUMMER MOPING ABOUT HER BOYFRIEND. SHE THINKS HE'S THE LOVE OF HER LIFE. ELLY, SHE DOESN'T EVEN KNOW WHAT LOVE IS !!!

DOES ANYBODY?

I DON'T UNDERSTAND IT, MRS. PATTERSON.

MY BOYFRIEND HAS NEVER WRITTEN OR PHONED ME-AND I MUST HAVE WRITTEN TO HIM A HUNDRED TIMES!!

BUT...MAYBE HE'S BEEN TOO BUSY, YOU KNOW. MAYBE HE'S FORGOTTEN. MAYBE HE JUST DOESN'T KNOW WHAT TO SAY!

MAYBE HE'S A JERK.

HOW CAN YOU SAY THAT?! HOW CAN YOU CALL MY BOYFRIEND A JERK WHEN YOU DON'T EVEN KNOW HIM?!!

WOULD YOU TREAT SOMEONE YOU LIKED THE WAY HE'S TREATING YOU?

NO.

SO KISS HIM GOODBYE AND...

I CAN'T!! HE MEANS EVERY-THING TO ME!!

HE'S GOT ALL MY DAVID BOWIE TAPES!!

SHE'LL GET OVER THIS BOY IN THUNDER BAY, CONNIE. I REMEMBER WHAT IT WAS LIKE TO BE A TEEN-AGER IN LOVE!

IN FACT.... I WAS IN SUCH A FOG ONCE, I COULDN'T SLEEP OR EAT —ALL I COULD THINK ABOUT WAS HIM. DAY AND NIGHT HE WAS ON MY MIND. I WROTE HIM POETRY, I COMPOSED SONGS....

WELL? DON'T JUST LEAVE THE STORY THERE! WHAT HAPPENED?!!!

I FAILED MATH.

23

MICHAEL! WHITE SHIRT? SHOES? PANTS?

EVERYONE'S WEARIN' WHITE, MA.

BUT YOU'RE GOING TO BE CHARGING AROUND A PLAYGROUND! YOU'RE.....

LIGHTEN UP, EL. THIS IS GRADE 6. KIDS IN GRADE 6 DON'T CHARGE AROUND THE PLAYGROUND!

...THEY LOITER.

AAAAGH!!! HOMEWORK ALREADY! WE'RE BACK ONE DAY AN' THEY'RE GIVING US HOMEWORK!!

NO FAIR! I HATE THIS! I WON'T DO IT!!

MIKE, IT'S SEPTEMBER. HOMEWORK IS PART OF SCHOOL, AND SCHOOL HAS STARTED.

I KNOW.

— BUT MY BRAINS ARE STILL ON HOLIDAY!!

GOSH, THIS IS QUITE A BIG HALL! I HAD NO IDEA SO MANY PEOPLE PLAYED BINGO!

SEE THAT SECOND TABLE ON THE LEFT THERE? WELL, I'M USUALLY 3 SEATS OVER, FACING THE CANTEEN.

WELL, I GUESS I COULD JOIN YOU FOR ONE GAME.

ONE GAME?

HONEY, ONCE YOU GET STARTED - YOU'RE HOOKED FOR LIFE !!!

Lynn

ONLY TWO CARDS? COME ON - YOU CAN HANDLE AT LEAST FOUR !!

LOOK, YOU FOLKS DON'T REALLY TAKE THIS GAME SERIOUSLY, DO YOU?

OH.

CANTEEN

BINGO CARDS

Lynn

FIRST GAME, TWO LINES IN ANY DIRECTION! OK, FOLKS, HERE WE GO - UNDER THE I, 17! I-17!

LET'S SEE ... I'VE GOT IT HERE, BUT ...

G-57! UNDER THE G, 57!

WAIT A MINUTE! I'VE GOT 4 CARDS HERE! I CAN'T KEEP UP !!

HONEY, IF YOU CAN'T DRIVE IN THE FAST LANE, GET OFF THE FREEWAY !!

Lynn

29

SO, YOU'RE REALLY ENJOYING THE NURSING HOME!

LET'S SAY I'M ADAPTING.

ACTUALLY... I HAVE A CONFESSION TO MAKE. I'VE MET A GENTLEMAN WHO REALLY STRIKES MY FANCY!

WE'VE BEEN SHARING THE SAME TABLE FOR THE LAST FEW DAYS, AND WHEN I LOOK INTO HIS EYES IT'S....

KA-POWIE!!!

ELLY, I HAVEN'T HAD A CRUSH ON SOMEONE FOR SO LONG... THIS IS WONDERFUL!

HE POKED ME WITH HIS CANE THIS MORNING, AND AN ELECTRIC CURRENT RAN THROUGH ME FROM HEAD TO TOE!

IT'S ALL THE SAME RUSH AND INTRIGUE AND EXCITEMENT THAT I FELT WHEN I WAS 20!

ISN'T IT NICE TO KNOW THAT SOME THINGS DON'T CHANGE?

HOW COULD I HAVE LET MRS. B. TALK ME INTO PLAYING A DUMB GAME LIKE BINGO?!

I SPENT AN ENTIRE EVENING SITTING THERE PUTTING LITTLE CHIPS ON LITTLE SQUARES.

HOW RIDICULOUS. HOW CAN ANYBODY SPEND ALL THAT TIME IN A SMOKY HALL PLAYING BINGO, FOR HEAVEN'S SAKE?!!!

......ALL I NEEDED WAS B-9. IF ONLY HE'D CALLED B-9!!!

30

SO- HOW'S OLD MRS. BAIRD?

MRS. BAIRD HAS A BOY-FRIEND!

WHAT? SHE'S 83 AND SHE HAS A BOYFRIEND? I THINK THAT'S FUNNY!

SHE DOESN'T. SHE SAYS THAT EVERY TIME HE'S NEAR, SHE CAN HARDLY BREATHE - AND HER HEART SKIPS A BEAT!

MAYBE SHE NEEDS A PACEMAKER.

YOU WOULDN'T BELIEVE IT, ANNIE. MRS. B. IS SO TAKEN WITH THIS GUY, SHE HAS STARS IN HER EYES!

WOULDN'T IT BE FUN TO BE WILDLY, MADLY, CRAZILY IN LOVE AGAIN?

TELL ME ABOUT IT.

DON'T YOU CONSIDER YOURSELF IN LOVE, ANNIE?

I GUESS SO.

BUT AFTER 10 YEARS OF MARRIAGE AND 3 KIDS... THERE'S NOT MUCH TO JUMP UP AND DOWN ABOUT.

SEEMS TO ME THAT IF YOU'RE NOT FALLING IN LOVE OR BREAKING UP, YOU JUST TAKE EACH OTHER FOR GRANTED.

.... LOVE BECOMES SORT OF A DIAL TONE HUM.

ELIZABETH, I ASKED YOU TO PICK UP THE TOYS ON THE FRONT LAWN!

I FORGOT.

LOOK AT THAT MESS!! YOUR ATTITUDE IS: "IF I WAIT LONG ENOUGH, SOMEONE ELSE WILL DO IT FOR ME."

I GUESS I DIDN'T WAIT LONG ENOUGH.

KNOW WHY YOUR MOM'S MAD AT YOU, LIZZIE? RICHARD TOLD ON YOU. THAT'S WHY.

HE SAW YOU IN THE PARK, WHEN YOU WERE SUPPOSED TO CLEAN UP, AN' HE WENT AN' TOLD ON YOU!

THAT DUMB RICHARD!!!

YEAH. IF THERE'S ANYTHING I HATE, IT'S SOMEONE WHO GOES AN' TATTLE TALES ON SOMEBODY ELSE!

NYAH, NYAH! I GOT ICE CREAM AN' YOU DON'T.

SO?

I GOT BANILLA AN' YOU CAN'T HAAAVE SOME!

WE REALLY DON'T CARE.

IF YOU'RE TRYING TO MAKE US JEALOUS, RICHARD, IT'S NOT GOING TO WORK.

WHAT DO YOU MEAN YOU HAVE TO HAVE ICE CREAM NOW?!

42

WHEN WE WERE KIDS, GROWING UP IN VANCOUVER, WE ALWAYS HAD FIREWORKS AT HALLOWE'EN.

AFTER WE WENT 'ROUND TO THE HOUSES, DAD WOULD SET THEM OFF IN THE FRONT YARD.

LEAVE ME ALONE, MIKE! GIMME MY BAG! I WANNA GO TRICK·OR·TREATING BY MYSELF!

YES...WHAT'S HALLOWE'EN WITHOUT FIREWORKS!

ELIZABETH, DADDY'S AT A MEETING, SO I WANT YOU TO GO OUT WITH MICHAEL TONIGHT.

YOU DON'T HAFTA WALK BESIDE ME, LIZZIE. I'LL WALK BEHIND YOU SO NOBODY WILL KNOW WE'RE TOGETHER.

OK.

THAT'S FAR ENOUGH!!

WELL, IT'S ABOUT TIME YOU TWO GOT IN... I WAS BEGINNING TO WORRY!

AW, MOM! — YOU WORRY ABOUT EVERY-THING!

WE WENT TRICK-OR-TREATING, AN' TOOK OUR TIME WALKING BACK! THAT'S ALL.

YEAH. — WE WANTED TO EAT SOME OF THE STUFF DAD LIKES BEFORE WE GOT HOME!

MICHAEL, WHAT IS THE GREEN COLORING YOU USED ON YOUR FACE?

FOOD DYE

FOOD DYE?!! — WHY DIDN'T YOU USE THE STAGE MAKE UP I BOUGHT FOR YOU?

BLFFTT

I DIDN'T LIKE ANY OF THE COLORS.

WELL, I HOPE YOU LIKE THE COLOR YOU'VE GOT....

I CAN'T GET IT OFF!

CAN'T GET IT OFF?!! BUT — I'VE GOT TO GO TO SCHOOL TOMORROW!!

I CAN'T GO TO SCHOOL WITH A GREEN FACE — I'LL DIE!!!

I'LL LOOK RIDICULOUS! EVERYONE WILL TEASE ME! — WHAT AM I GONNA DO?!!

FIND A SHIRT TO MATCH?

Panel 1: GOOD MORNING, GENTLEMEN. I TRUST YOU HAVE AN EXPLANATION.

Panel 2: WELL, WE WERE IN THE WASHROOM, BECAUSE MICHAEL HAD TO, UH... WASH.
I SEE.

Panel 3: AND-ARE WE ALL SQUEAKY CLEAN? ARE WE KISSING SWEET? ARE WE ALL REFRESHED AND READY TO START A BRAND NEW DAY? OH, GOOOD!!

Panel 4: SARCASM: THE RAZOR STRAP OF THE '80S.

Panel 5: NOW, WE FOLLOW THE VOLGA DOWN INTO THE CASPIAN SEA. HERE AT THE BORDER BETWEEN...

Panel 6: MICHAEL PATTERSON! WHAT IS THE PRESENT NAME OF THE COUNTRY THAT WAS ONCE CALLED "PERSIA"?
UH?

Panel 7: DID I WAKE YOU UP? OH, DEAR. SILLY ME!

Panel 8: ONCE AGAIN, I'VE MISTAKEN A GLAZED STARE FOR A LOOK OF KEEN INTEREST!

Panel 9: GORDON... I DON'T FEEL GOOD!
YOU'RE KIDDIN' ME.

Panel 10: BELIEVE IT, MAN! - I'VE GOT A STOMACH ACHE AN' A FEVER.

Panel 11: WHAT IS IT, PATTERSON?! - IS THERE SOMETHING YOU'D LIKE TO SHARE WITH THE CLASS?
YES, SIR.

Panel 12: ...IT'S THE FLU.

THE SCHOOL SECRETARY IS ON THE PHONE, ELLY— MICHAEL'S COME DOWN WITH THE FLU!

WHAT? THAT MEANS I HAVE TO DRIVE ALL THE WAY DOWN TO THE WEST END! I'LL MISS MY MEETING AT LUNCH!!

WHAT A PAIN! WHY DO THEY ALWAYS GET SICK ON A DAY WHEN I'M UP TO MY NECK IN CHAOS?!!

SHE'LL TAKE YOUR CALL IN A MINUTE. MRS. PATTERSON GETS SO EMOTIONAL WHEN HER KIDS ARE ILL.

I'M SORRY. I FELT OK WHEN I LEFT THIS MORNING. IT'S NOT MY FAULT THAT I GOT THE FLU!

HEY, CAN WE PICK UP SOME VIDEOS ON THE WAY HOME?

VIDEOS?!

MICHAEL, IF YOU'RE TOO SICK TO GO TO SCHOOL, YOU'RE TOO SICK TO WATCH MOVIES!!

WHAT AM I SUPPOSED TO DO... GO TO BED?

HERE, TAKE THIS COLD MEDICINE AND SLEEP FOR A WHILE.

...DON'T FEEL LIKE SLEEP-ING.

AT LEAST LIE DOWN, THEN! AND PUT SOMETHING WARM ON YOUR FEET! YOU'RE GOING TO CATCH SOMETHING ELSE IF YOU KEEP WANDERING AROUND THE HOUSE LIKE THAT!!

I KNOW... (HACK, HACK, WHEEZE)

...I THINK I JUST PICKED UP A "NAGGING" COUGH!

I THINK I'LL GO BACK TO WORK NOW, HONEY— WILL YOU BE OK?

SURE. I'LL (COUGH)... MANAGE. MY FEVER MIGHT GO DOWN, AND I THINK I CAN PUT UP WITH THE PAIN.

MICHAEL, IF YOU WANT ME TO STAY HOME— SAY SO!!

.....IT'S UP TO YOU.

WHY DO I RESENT HAVING TO STAY HOME WITH MICHAEL? WHEN HE WAS LITTLE AND WAS SICK, I'D DROP EVERY- THING TO LOOK AFTER HIM.

MAYBE IT'S BECAUSE THEY REALLY NEED YOU WHEN THEY'RE LITTLE. ...HE DOESN'T SEEM TO NEED ME ANY MORE.

MOM?

UH HUH.

NOTHING. JUST MAKING SURE YOU WERE STILL THERE.

YESSIR, SHE'S A LITTLE BEAUTY! HAVE WE GOT A DEAL?

WELL, HEH, I'M NOT TOO SURE. SHE'S NICE—BUT TOO IMPRACTICAL FOR A FAMILY MAN.

I UNDERSTAND.

YOU'RE LETTING HIM GO? JUST LIKE THAT?

HE'LL BE BACK.

....HE LEFT LIP PRINTS ON THE HOOD.

I SHOULDN'T DO THIS... I'LL CANCEL MY APPOINTMENT WITH THE BANK.

PAT PAT

BUT—IF I TRADE IN MY SEDAN, I WON'T NEED A BIG LOAN....

FUMBLE FUMBLE

WHAT'S ON YOUR MIND, DOC? YOU SEEM PREOCCUPIED!

WHY?

...YOU LEFT YOUR PEN IN THE AUTOCLAVE.

AUTOCLAVE HOT STERILIZATION

DRIVING GLOVES? YES, SIR.

TWEED CAP?

I THINK SO.

RED CASHMERE SCARF?

OF COURSE.

I'M NOT JUST BUYING A CAR... I'M BUYING A LIFESTYLE!

CONGRATULATIONS! AND BELIEVE ME, YOU WON'T REGRET BUYING THIS LITTLE HONEY!

MY WIFE WILL KILL ME!! NOW, THAT'S THE WRONG ATTITUDE.

LOOK, WHAT DOES A WOMAN DO WHEN SHE NEEDS A LITTLE PICK-ME-UP?...SHE GOES SHOPPING, RIGHT? SHE BUYS HERSELF SOMETHING, RIGHT?

SO, YOU TELL HER ALL YOU DID WAS WHAT SHE'D DO! YOU BOUGHT YOURSELF A LITTLE PRESENT!

OH, NO! HE DID IT! HE BOUGHT THAT CAR!!

CONNIE, WHY WOULD A PERFECTLY RATIONAL MAN BUY A MACHINE LIKE THAT?

SIMPLE, EL.

IT'S A SYMBOL OF PROWESS! MEN NEVER STOP TRYING TO PROVE THEIR VIRILITY!

DON'T BE RIDICULOUS.

HONEY? COME ON OUTSIDE AND MEET THE NEW BABY!!

IT'S OURS? IT'S REALLY OURS? OH, WOW!!

I KNOW IT WASN'T A SENSIBLE PURCHASE, EL, BUT...

IT'S OK. I DON'T MIND.

YOU DON'T?! YOU'RE NOT MAD THAT I TRADED MY CAR IN ON A USELESS IMPRACTICAL CAR LIKE THAT?

NOPE.

AS LONG AS YOU'RE THE ONE WHO'LL BE DRIVING IT ALL WINTER!

OH.

MICHAEL... YOU KNOW HOW MOM SAID IF YOU PUT LIQUID SOAP IN THE DISHWASHER, IT WOULD FOAM ALL OVER THE PLACE?

UH HUH

WELL, SHE WAS RIGHT.

ELIZABETH, WHAT ARE YOU DOING IN THE KITCHEN?

PLAYING.

THERE'S WATER, AND FLOUR, AND CHOCOLATE SPRINKLES EVERY- WHERE!

WHAT'S THE MATTER WITH YOU? CAN'T MOM LEAVE YOU ALONE FOR 10 MINUTES?

UH- HUH.

... BUT SHE'S BEEN GONE FOR AN HOUR AND A HALF!

SANTA'S WATCHING YOU, LIZZIE.

IS NOT.

SANTA'S GOT A MAGIC MIRROR, AND HE'S WATCHING EVERY- THING YOU DO.

HAS NOT.

THEN HOW DO YOU THINK HE KNOWS ABOUT ALL THE DUMB THINGS YOU DO?!!

SANTA'S GOT A FINK.

LOOK! I GOT NINE DOLLARS AN' ELEVEN CENTS TO SPEND ON CHRISTMAS!

YOU CAN'T BUY SOMETHING FOR EVERYONE WITH NINE DOLLARS AN' ELEVEN CENTS, LIZZIE!

I'M GONNA TRY!

WELL, THEY'RE SURE GONNA BE CHEAP PRESENTS.

NOTHING IS CHEAP, MICHAEL, IF IT COSTS ALL THE MONEY YOU HAVE!!

WHAT ARE YOU DRAWING?

REINDEER.

DOESN'T LOOK LIKE REINDEER. WHAT'S ALL THE BLUE STUFF?

THAT'S RAIN, DEAR!

AN OLDIE IS NOT NECESSARILY A GOODIE, ELIZABETH.

WANNA COME IN OUTTA THE SNOW, FARLEY?

NO!! DON'T SHAKE!

60

THIS ONE! THIS ONE! I WANT THIS ONE!!

CHRISTMAS TREE!

AGH! MFF! OWWWW!!

YOU CAN'T HUG A CHRISTMAS TREE, ELIZABETH!

LYNN

NEW YEAR'S EVE? ...I DON'T KNOW, ROY, WE DON'T HAVE A BABY SITTER.

I'LL BABY-SIT! I'M OLD ENOUGH! I'M RELIABLE AN' HONEST—ASK ANYBODY!!

MICHAEL IS A RAT-FINK!!

WHO ASKED YOU?!!

...UH I'LL CALL YOU BACK.

I MUST BE GETTING OLD OR SOMETHING, EL, BUT I'D RATHER STAY HOME THAN GO TO A PARTY.

MY IDEA OF A GREAT TIME WAS ALWAYS SPENDING NEW YEAR'S EVE WITH THE PEOPLE YOU LIKE THE BEST...

—AND THE PEOPLE I LIKE BEST ARE RIGHT HERE!

DAD AND I HAVE DECIDED TO STAY HOME, GUYS—WE'RE GOING TO SEE THE NEW YEAR IN TOGETHER!

WE THOUGHT THAT A GOOD NEW YEAR'S RESOLUTION WOULD BE TO SPEND MORE TIME WITH OUR KIDS!

HOW COME?

BECAUSE WE'RE THE ONLY PARENTS YOU RELATE TO THAT AREN'T ON TELEVISION.

THIS IS GOING TO BE A LATE NIGHT, YOU TWO .... GO AND GET INTO YOUR PAJAMAS.

TWELVE O'CLOCK IS WAY PAST YOUR BEDTIME, AND YOU'RE GOING TO BE DEAD TIRED—SO I WANT YOU READY FOR BED.

FIVE! FOUR! THREE! TWO! ONE....

HAPPY NEW YEAR, ELIZABETH.

WOW! IT'S A WHOLE NEW YEAR! 1988!!

'88 IS REALLY GREAT! I COULDN'T WAIT FOR '88!
'88 LET'S MAKE A DATE! DON'T BE LATE— IT'S '88!!

YES... IT'S GOING TO BE A GREAT YEAR FOR ADVERTISING.

THE KIDS AND I TOOK THE TREE DOWN, HONEY... AND WHAT WE'D LIKE TO KNOW IS....

HOW DO YOU GET ALL THAT STUFF INTO THOSE LITTLE TINY BOXES?

66

WELL, GOOD FOR IRENE. BETTER TO GO IT ALONE THAN TO STICK WITH A GUY LIKE TED.

HE GOT WHAT HE DESERVED. EVERYONE KNEW HE WAS FOOLING AROUND ON HER.

IF EVERYONE KNEW HE WAS FOOLING AROUND, HOW COME NOBODY TOLD HER?!!

WHAT—AND RUIN THEIR RELATIONSHIP?

SO... IRENE AND TED SPLIT UP, DID THEY.

WAS IT BECAUSE HE WAS SEEING ANOTHER WOMAN?

UH-HUH

WELL... I'M NOT SURPRISED.

WHY?

BECAUSE WHEN I WAS ENGAGED TO TED... IRENE WAS THE OTHER WOMAN!

MARRIAGES NEVER USED TO SPLIT UP, JOHN. MARRIAGES USED TO LAST FOREVER.

I WONDER IF MODERN THINKING MAKES PEOPLE MORE LIKELY TO LEAVE A MARRIAGE THAN TO STAY AND TRY TO WORK THINGS OUT.

... IF ANYTHING HAPPENED BETWEEN US, JOHN, WOULD YOU WANT TO STAY AND WORK THINGS OUT?

SURE.

SOMETIMES IT'S BETTER TO SALVAGE AN OLD BARGE THAN TO TRY BUILDING A NEW ONE.

DRY DRY DRY DRY!

GEL GEL GEL GEL

STYLE STYLE STYLE STYLE

WHAP WHAP! WHAP WHAP!!

I'M TAKING YOUR CAR THIS MORNING, HONEY. MINE'S NO GOOD IN THIS WEATHER.

MY CAR?

WAIT A MINUTE! WHEN YOU BOUGHT THAT SILLY SPORTS CAR, YOU TOLD ME NOT TO WORRY!

YOU SAID YOU COULD DRIVE IT ALL WINTER! YOU SAID IT WAS AN ALL-WEATHER VEHICLE!

SO?... IT'S A SOME WEATHER VEHICLE!!

JOHN, IF YOU TAKE MY CAR, HOW AM I GOING TO GET TO WORK?

MY COLUMN HAS TO GO TO THE PAPER, THEY'RE EXPECTING ME AT THE LIBRARY AND....

I'LL DELIVER THE COLUMN EL, AND YOU'RE PART TIME—YOU CAN SKIP WORK FOR A DAY!!

WHAT?

LOOK, WHOSE JOB IS MORE IMPORTANT—YOURS OR MINE?

71

ELLY!! IS THAT YOU? ... CONNIE?

WHAT A STORM! MY CAR'S IN A DITCH, THEY'VE CLOSED THE STREETS, CANCELED SCHOOL BUSES...

WE MIGHT NOT SEE OUR KIDS OR OUR HUSBANDS FOR HOURS! WHAT SHOULD WE DO?

RED WINE OR WHITE?

AWESOME, MAN! THERE'S SO MUCH SNOW COMING DOWN, YOU CAN'T SEE A THING!!

WHAT IF WE CAN'T GET HOME? WHAT IF WE HAFTA SPEND THE WHOLE NIGHT AT SCHOOL? IT COULD HAPPEN!

ASK MR. WARREN, AND SEE WHAT HE THINKS.

I DID.

HE'S THINKING.

THAT WAS GREG. HE AND JOHN HAVE CHECKED INTO A HOTEL.

THAT'S A RELIEF!

THIS AWFUL STORM! STREETS CLOSED, KIDS STUCK AT SCHOOL—HOW LONG IS IT GOING TO GO ON LIKE THIS?

DON'T WORRY, EL. IT COULD BE WORSE! AT LEAST THE POWER HASN'T GONE...

OFF.

GOSH, THE HOUSE IS COLD. I SHOULD HAVE LEFT CONNIE'S PLACE AGES AGO!

CLICK!

WITH THE WORST OF THE STORM OVER, HYDRO WORKERS ARE DOING ALL THEY CAN TO RESTORE POWER TO THE AREA.

IN THE MEANTIME, LIGHT THE CANDLES—HERE'S SOME ROMANTIC MUSIC FOR YOU AND "THAT SOMEONE SPECIAL" TO CUDDLE UP TO.

KISS ME AND YOU'RE DEAD MEAT.

HEY, MAN—THE SNOW'S STOPPED!

YEAH!

LOOK, THE SNOW PLOW IS OUT THERE! AN' A COUPLE OF GUYS ON SNOWMOBILES!

WE'RE SAVED!

MR. WARREN! THE STORM'S OVER! THE BUSES ARE HERE! WE DON'T HAVE TO STAY AT SCHOOL ALL NIGHT!

YES... I BELIEVE THERE IS POWER IN PRAYER.

OK, EVERYONE ON EASTBOUND BUS 17, LINE UP OVER HERE, PLEASE!

LOOKIT THAT, ELIZABETH! A FEW HOURS AGO, WE WERE IN THE MIDDLE OF A BLIZZARD, AN' NOW THE STARS ARE OUT!

...IT'S AS IF THE STORM NEVER HAPPENED!

RRRRR   SHOVEL

SHOVEL SHOVEL   SCRAPE SCRAPE

BOY, I'VE NEVER SEEN A STORM LIKE THAT IN MY LIFE!

ME TOO!

YOU WOULDN'T BELIEVE HOW BAD THE ROADS ARE, MOM. ON THE WAY HOME WE SAW A CAR IN THE DITCH THAT LOOKED EXACTLY LIKE OURS!

OH.

THE POWER'S STILL OFF, SO WE'RE SLEEPING IN THE LIVING ROOM TONIGHT.

DO WE HAFTA?

PRETEND IT'S THE OLDEN DAYS. WE'RE IN A COLD STONE COTTAGE ON A SCOTTISH HILLSIDE. WE HUDDLE TO KEEP WARM AS AN ICY WIND WHISTLES ACROSS THE MOOR!

HARK! I HEAR BAGPIPES!!

THAT WAS MY STOMACH. ...LIE DOWN!

IN A WAY, I'M SORRY WE DIDN'T HAFTA SPEND THE WHOLE NIGHT AT SCHOOL.

AFTER THE LIGHTS WENT OUT, IT WAS SORT OF SCARY... LIKE AN AIR RAID OR SOMETHING.

THINGS LIKE THAT SURE CHANGE PEOPLE SOMEHOW. AN EMERGENCY MAKES THINGS DIFFERENT.

JUST FOR A WHILE TODAY... EVERYONE CARED ABOUT EVERYONE ELSE.

80

THEN I GO, "WELLL?," AN' THEN HE GOES (TOTALLY WEIRD) I MEAN, HE GOES-" SO, WHAT AM I SUPPOSED TO SAY?!!" RIGHT?

AND THEN I GO," YOU KNOW." AN' THEN HE GOES (LIKE, YOU KNOW, WITH THIS TOTALLY AWESOME LOOK), HE GOES, "RIIIIIGHT."

IS HER CONVERSATION ALWAYS LIKE THAT?

THAT'S THE WAY SHE GOES!

I'M GOING OUT, CONNIE.

WHERE ARE YOU GOING, AND WHEN WILL YOU BE BACK?

OH, JEEZ! OK, I'M GOING TO THE MALL. I'LL BE BACK BY 10.

TRY 9:30.

9:30?! THAT'S ONLY 2 HOURS! I MEAN THAT'S TOTALLY UNFAIR! FINE-HAVE IT YOUR WAY! IF I HAFTA BE IN BY 9:30, THEN I'M NOT GOING TO GO OUT AT ALL!!!

TRANSLATION: "I REALLY DIDN'T WANT TO GO OUT ANYWAY."

LIVING WITH TEEN-AGERS IS A WHOLE NEW GAME, EL.

BEING A PARENT TO MOLLY AND GAYLE IS THE HARDEST THING I'VE EVER DONE.

OH, WELL, SOMEDAY WE'LL ALL GET ALONG. I KEEP TELLING MYSELF THERE'S A LIGHT AT THE END OF THE TUNNEL!

...I JUST HOPE THAT IT DOESN'T NEED BATTERIES!

HERE'S YOUR STUFF FROM THE CORNER STORE, MRS. P. THERE'S FOUR DOLLARS CHANGE.

THANKS, GAYLE! YOU'RE A SWEET KID.

I KNOW.

...THAT'S MY PROBLEM.

NOBODY EVER NOTICES ME, MRS. PATTERSON. ...I'M JUST A "NICE KID."

BUT EVERYBODY NOTICES MOLLY! THEY'RE ALWAYS TALKING ABOUT HER—ALWAYS WORRYING ABOUT HER...

MY SISTER THROWS A 6-MONTH FIT WHEN WE MOVE, SHE SPIKES HER HAIR, ACTS LIKE A CREEP, STARTS DATING GEEKS 'N' EVERYONE FALLS ALL OVER HER!!

MAYBE I'M LIVING MY LIFE ALL WRONG.

YOU DON'T WANT TO BE LIKE MOLLY, DO YOU?

I DON'T KNOW HOW I WANT TO BE.

SOMETIMES I LOOK IN THE MIRROR AND I SEE THIS FACE AND I DON'T HAVE ANY IDEA ABOUT WHO I AM OR WHAT I AM.

I USED TO FEEL THAT WAY WHEN I WAS YOUR AGE.....AND YOU KNOW WHAT?

I THINK I'M FINALLY STARTING TO FIGURE IT OUT!

KNOW WHAT WE SHOULD DO TO PULL YOU OUT OF THIS MOOD, KIDDO? WE SHOULD MAKE YOU OVER!

WE'LL CHANGE YOUR HAIR, FIND YOU A WILD COLOR TO WEAR, AND SPIFF YOU UP A LITTLE!

THERE!

WOW! SHOULD I PUT SOMETHING ON MY FACE?

SURE!..... PUT A SMILE ON IT.

LOOK WHAT MIKE'S MOM DID, LAWRENCE! SHE BRAIDED MY HAIR, AN' GAVE ME THIS RED SWEATER!

PRETTY NEAT, GAYLE!

YEAH!

YOU SURE THAT'S MY MOM'S RED SWEATER?

UH HUH.

BOY! SO THAT'S HOW IT'S SUPPOSED TO LOOK!

GAYLE, NEXT DOOR, SAID THAT NOBODY EVER PAYS ANY ATTENTION TO HER, JOHN....

SO TODAY I FUSSED OVER HER, DID UP HER HAIR AND MADE HER FEEL MUCH BETTER ABOUT HERSELF!

THAT'S GREAT, EL!

WELL, I DON'T THINK IT'S SO GREAT.

WHY NOT, ELIZABETH?

'CAUSE ALL THE TIME YOU WERE PAYIN' ATTENTION TO HER.... YOU NEVER PAID ANY ATTENTION TO ME!!

HERE, DAD....

I WANT YOU TO LISTEN TO SOMETHING GOOD FOR A CHANGE!

MICHAEL, I PUT A PILE OF CLEAN LAUNDRY IN YOUR ROOM. DID YOU PUT IT AWAY?

NOT YET.

LOOK AT THIS MESS! I DON'T KNOW HOW YOU CAN LIVE IN HERE!!

BEDDING, CLOTHES ALL OVER THE PLACE! YOU CAN'T TELL WHICH CLOTHES ARE CLEAN AND WHICH ARE DIRTY!!

CAN SO.

...THE CLEAN PILE HASN'T BEEN WALKED ON.

MOM, CAN I BORROW A DOLLAR?

NOT A CHANCE.

AWW, COME ON— JUST A BUCK! I'LL PAY IT BACK OUTA MY ALLOWANCE!

MICHAEL, YOU HAVEN'T HAD YOUR ALLOWANCE FOR 2 WEEKS, AND YOU WON'T GET IT UNTIL YOU CLEAN YOUR ROOM!

OH.

...CAN I HAVE AN ADVANCE ON MY INHERITANCE?

HEY, ELIZABETH, CAN I BORROW A DOLLAR?

I DUNNO.

LOOK. I'LL GIVE YOU THIS TO KEEP 'TILL I CAN PAY IT BACK!

WELL... OK.

I JUST SAW MIKE HEADING FOR THE STORE, ELLY. HE'S NOT SUPPOSED TO HAVE ANY MONEY 'TIL HE CLEANS HIS ROOM! THAT'S THE RULE!!!

THERE WAS A LOOPHOLE.

....HE PAWNED HIS TEDDY.

YE-AAGHH!

WHAT THE HECK WAS THAT?

I IGNORED SOMETHING .....AND IT DIDN'T GO AWAY.

I CAN'T STAND IT, CONNIE. EVERY TIME I GO PAST MICHAEL'S ROOM, I WANT TO SCREAM!

LOOK, EL, IF HE TIDIED HIS ROOM, HE'D BE CONFORMING TO YOUR STANDARDS. BY LIVING IN A PIGSTY, THESE KIDS ARE PROCLAIMING THEIR INDEPENDENCE!

THEY'RE SHOWING YOU THAT THEY HAVE THEIR OWN MINDS, THAT THEY ARE SEPARATE, UNIQUE INDIVIDUALS!

KIDS!!

YEAH.... THEY'RE ALL ALIKE.

LOOKIT, MOM — I GOT MY TOOF ALMOST OUT!

I CAN PUSH MY TONGUE UNDER IT.... THEE?

WIGGLE WIGGLE PUSH POKE WIGGLE PULL

WHY DO THEY ALWAYS DO THIS AT DINNER?

AH! I GOT IT OUT! I PULLED OUT MY TOOF! SEE?

WAY TA GO, LIZ!

HEY! NOW YOU CAN EAT PEAS ONE AT A TIME WITHOUT OPENIN' YOUR MOUTH! YOU CAN STICK A STRAW IN THERE, AN' FIRE SPITBALLS WITHOUT TAKIN' IT OUT TO RELOAD...

MICHAEL...THAT IS ENOUGH !!!

WHAT'S WRONG? I'M ONLY GIVING HER THE BENEFIT OF MY EXPERIENCE!

CAN I HAVE THIS BOX, MICHAEL?

NOPE. 'CAUSE I WANT IT.

NO FAIR! MEANIE! YOU ONLY WANT IT 'CAUSE I WANT IT! AAAUGH!! I'M TELLING!!!

OK. HERE. YOU CAN HAVE IT, THEN.

I CAN?

HOW COME YOU DIDN'T JUST GIVE IT TO ME BEFORE?

....IT WAS TOO EASY.

I DON'T THINK YOU SHOULD TRY AND FOOL THE TOOTH FAIRY, LIZ. NOBODY'S EVER SEEN HER—NOT EVEN ME... AND I'M A DENTIST!

OH.

SO LET'S GO FIND YOUR TOOTH AND PUT IT UNDER YOUR PILLOW.

CAN'T GET IT NOW, DADDY.

WHY NOT? YOU COULDN'T HAVE HIDDEN IT THAT WELL!

UH HUH.

I SWALLOWED IT!!!

SHE WHAT?!!

SHE SWALLOWED IT.

I GUESS SHE WAS TRYING TO FIT HER TOOTH INTO THE SPACE IT CAME OUT OF... AND IT JUST WENT DOWN!

I TOLD HER THE TOOTH FAIRY WOULD STILL COME, BUT SHE'S PRETTY UPSET. IT'S AFTER 10 AND SHE'S WIDE AWAKE... WHAT HAPPENS NOW?

THE TOOTH FAIRY WILL THINK HORRIBLE THOUGHTS ABOUT CHILDREN, AND SET HER ALARM CLOCK FOR 2 A.M.

UH, EL? IT'S 2:15. HAS THE TOOTH FAIRY BEEN TO SEE ELIZABETH YET?

GRUNT.

WAS THAT AN AFFIRMATIVE GRUNT, A NEGATIVE GRUNT OR AN UNDECIDED GRUNT?

MPH.

AHA! IT'S AN AFFIRMATIVE GRUNT!

YOU KNOW YOU'VE BEEN MARRIED A LONG TIME WHEN YOU START TAKING EACH OTHER FOR GRUNTED!

SHE CAME! THE TOOF FAIRY REALLY CAME!

ISN'T THAT NICE, LIZZIE!

KNOW WHAT I THINK, MOM? I THINK THERE'S MORE THAN ONE TOOF FAIRY IN THE WORLD.

....AN' I HOPE WE GET A DIFF'RENT ONE NEXT TIME.

WHY'S THAT, HONEY?

'CAUSE THE ONE THAT WENT TO MELODY'S HOUSE GAVE HER 50¢ .... AND I ONLY GOT A QUARTER.

THE TOOTH FAIRY LEFT YOU A QUARTER? HEY, EASY MONEY, MAN! EASY MONEY!

SCREECH!

WHAT IS GOING ON?!

NOTHING. LIZZIE SAID SHE GOT A QUARTER FROM THE TOOTH FAIRY...

—AN' I SHOWED HER HOW SHE COULD MAKE A BUCK!

THERE'S MY LITTLE ONE WITH A SEVEN-YEAR-OLD'S GAP-TOOTHED SMILE.

THEY CALL THIS THE "UGLY DUCKLING" STAGE.

.... BUT, OH, ELIZABETH!

... DON'T TURN INTO A SWAN TOO SOON!!

BOY, I HOPE WE WIN TONIGHT! I WANT THIS TO BE THE BEST GAME OF THE SEASON!

IT DOESN'T MATTER WHAT THE OUTCOME OF THE GAME IS, MIKE— IT'S STILL GOING TO BE THE BEST GAME OF THE SEASON!

HOW COME?

BECAUSE IT'S THE LAST GAME OF THE SEASON!!

WATCH YOUR DRINK, NOW, DON'T SPILL IT'!

EXCUSE ME. PARDON ME.

I SAID KEEP THE LID ON THAT DRINK!

PARDON ME, THANK YOU...

MAKE SURE THAT DRINK IS.... ELIZABETH, WHERE ARE YOU GOING?

I THINK I DROPPED MY WEENIE IN THE 3RD ROW!

SKATE, MIKE!! SKATE SKATE, SKATE!!!

UH...MOM?

GET IN THERE, MIKE! GO FOR IT! SKATE!!

MOM?

GO, MIKE! SKATE SK... UH, WHAT IS IT, ELIZABETH?

MICHAEL'S STILL ON THE BENCH.

OK, GUYS, WE'RE GONNA GET SERIOUS! I WANT YOU TO GET IN THERE AN' GIVE IT ALL YOU'VE GOT!!

WE'RE NOT THINKING NUMBERS HERE, WE'RE THINKING TEAM! WE'RE THINKING WIN! WE'RE THINKING COOPERATION!

BUT, COACH... THEY'RE LEADING 7 TO 3 .... AN' THERE'S ONLY 9 MINUTES LEFT IN THE GAME!

... WE'RE THINKING NUMBERS.

WELL, THAT'S IT... WE LOST THE TOURNAMENT.

WE WERE SO CLOSE! WE WERE THAT FAR FROM WINNING! .... COACH IS REALLY UPSET.

COME ON, MIKE. YOUR COACH KNOWS IT'S JUST A GAME! ... GROWN MEN DON'T TAKE THINGS LIKE THIS TOO SERIOUSLY!

WE'LL BE HOME LATER, EL. I'M GOING OUT WITH THE COACH AND THE BOYS FOR A ROOT BEER!

WELL, GUYS - I'M PROUD OF YOU! YOU WORKED HARD. — TO A GREAT GAME!! — TO A GREAT TEAM!!

SORRY YOU DIDN'T WIN, MIKE?

NOPE!

THIS IS THE PART I LIKE BEST ANYWAYS.

WE SAID WE'D PAY YOU SOMETHING FOR CLEANING UP THE BACK YARD, MIKE. ....HERE'S $2.00

TWO BUCKS?!! BUT I WORKED FOR OVER AN HOUR! THIS IS LESS THAN MINIMUM WAGE!!

YOU DID LESS THAN MINIMUM WORK.

WORK, WORK, WORK— THAT'S ALL YOU EVER WANT ME TO DO!

IT'S NO FAIR!!

I'M A KID, MAN! KIDS ARE SUPPOSED TO HAVE FUN! WHY CAN'T YOU WAIT 'TIL I'M GROWN UP?

THEN I'LL WORK !!!

THAT'S AN IDEA, MIKE, BUT IT'S NOT A GOOD ONE.

WHY NOT?

BECAUSE BY THE TIME YOU'RE GROWN UP AND READY TO WORK ...YOU WON'T KNOW HOW!

THAT SURE IS A WEIRD DUDE MOLLY'S HANGIN' OUT WITH. WHERE'D SHE MEET HIM — IN A MORGUE?

SHE MET HIM AT A ROCK CONCERT, MAN! HE'S LEAD GUITARIST FOR THE EMETIX!

NO KIDDING! IS HE SOME KINDA STAR?

NOPE...BUT HE ONCE MOONED AN AUDIENCE IN OAKVILLE!

HEY, MAN—YOU PLAY FOR THE EMETIX? GREAT GROUP! I SAW YOU GUYS ON TV!

HEAVY METAL, RIGHT? GREAT SOUND! I, UH...COULD I HAVE YOUR AUTOGRAPH?

SURE. WHY NOT.

....I DIDN'T HAVE ANY PAPER.

OH, DEAR. I'D HOPED MOLLY WOULD DATE A NICE, ORDINARY GUY, EL.

HE'S PROBABLY A NICE KID, CONNIE—AND MOLLY'S NO SLOUCH! LET THE RELATIONSHIP RUN ITS COURSE. I WOULDN'T WORRY!

HE'S GOT A CAR.

I'D WORRY.

ISN'T DIRK WONDERFUL, GAYLE? HE'S SO DRAMATIC! SO DIVERSE!

HE'S INTO HEAVY METAL, ASTRAL PROJECTION AND TEN PIN BOWLING!

GOSH!

I'VE NEVER KNOWN ANYBODY LIKE HIM—AND WE HAVE SO MUCH IN COMMON!

LIKE?

NOBODY UNDERSTANDS ME EITHER.

I DON'T WANT YOU TWO GOING OUT TONIGHT... YOU HAVE HOMEWORK, AND YOUR ROOMS ARE A MESS!

OH, COME ON, DAD! THAT'S NO FAIR! YOU'VE GOT TO BE KIDDING! HOW CAN YOU DO THIS?

LOOK, ALL THIS TIME YOU'VE SPENT ARGUING COULD HAVE BEEN USED TO GET SOMETHING DONE!

AAACH!

SLAM!!

I LOVE COMING TO YOUR HOUSE, CONNIE.

...IT'S SO MUCH LIKE HOME!

WELL, NOBODY TOLD US THAT BEING A PARENT WAS GOING TO BE EASY!

YEAH.

WE KNEW WHAT WE WERE DOING WHEN WE MADE OUR DECISION, AND ALL WE CAN DO IS OUR BEST.

ABSOLUTELY.

AND SOMEDAY THEY'LL APPRECIATE US, EL! SOMEDAY THEY'LL KNOW HOW MUCH WE'VE DONE FOR THEM!

RIGHT!

SOMEDAY THEY'LL HAVE CHILDREN OF THEIR OWN!!

HAPPY BIRTHDAY TO YOUUUU HAPPY BIRTHDAY, DEAR MICHAEL, HAPPY BIRTHDAY TO YOUUUU

OK-NOW, MAKE A WISH AND BLOW OUT THE CANDLES!

THE BIGGER THE KID, THE BIGGER THE WISH.

A SLEEPOVER! HOW DID I EVER LET HIM TALK ME INTO A SLEEPOVER?!!

SIX ADOLESCENT BOYS TEARING UP MY REC ROOM, CONNIE! ...WHY DO I DO THIS TO MYSELF?!!

EL-I DON'T THINK YOU HAVE ENOUGH STRESS IN YOUR LIFE.

GUESS WHAT, ELIZABETH, I'M ALMOST TWO TIMES AS OLD AS YOU. I'M BIGGER THAN YOU, I'M SMARTER THAN YOU AND....

MICHAEL, I NEED YOU TO HELP CLEAN UP THE REC ROOM AND MOVE THE SOFA.

WE'LL BE EXPECTING A LOT MORE OF YOU NOW THAT YOU'RE TWELVE.

... BEING YOUNGER HAS ITS ADVANTAGES.

OH, WOW! A SLEEPOVER! IS THIS EVER GONNA BE FUN!

WHAT'S THAT—A PILLOW? HEY, GUYS! LAWRENCE BROUGHT A SECURITY PILLOW!

IT'S NOT A SECURITY PILLOW!

WHAT IS IT THEN?

SELF-DEFENSE!

WHAP!

CUT IT OUT!! I SAID STOP THAT!!

OK, GUYS—ONE MORE PILLOW FIGHT AND SO HELP ME, THERE WILL BE BIG TROUBLE!

WELL... I GUESS WE ALL KNOW WHAT THAT MEANS.

YEAH...

WE GET ONE MORE PILLOW FIGHT!!!

I KNOW YOU FEEL LEFT OUT, HONEY, BUT THIS IS MICHAEL'S PARTY, THOSE ARE HIS FRIENDS, AND I GUESS HE JUST DOESN'T WANT HIS LITTLE SISTER HANGING AROUND!

SOMEDAY IT WILL BE YOUR TURN! SOME DAY WE'LL HAVE A SLEEP-OVER, AND INVITE YOUR FRIENDS!

I GUESS SHE COULDN'T WAIT FOR "SOME-DAY."

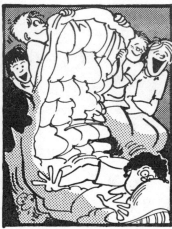

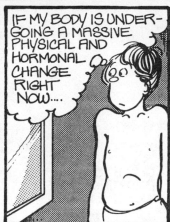

THE PROBLEM WITH ADOLESCENCE, MIKE, IS THAT EVERYONE'S CHANGING PHYSICALLY—BUT YOU'RE ALL CHANGING AT DIFFERENT RATES.

SOME BOYS GROW BEARDS EARLIER THAN OTHERS, SOME VOICES CRACK, AND OTHERS JUST DEEPEN SLOWLY....

DID YOU WORRY A LOT ABOUT THE CHANGES THAT WERE HAPPENING TO YOU WHEN YOU WERE A KID, DAD?

NAH.

I WAS TOO BUSY NOTICING THE CHANGES THAT HAPPENED TO THE GIRLS!!

THAT'S IT! I'VE GONE THROUGH EVERY RACK OF BATHING SUITS I CAN FIND—AND THEY'RE ALL THE SAME!!

WHY DO THEY KEEP MAKING THESE AWFUL THINGS? WHY ARE THEY DOING THIS TO US?!!

THEY'RE NOT DOING IT TO US, EL...WE'RE DOING IT TO OURSELVES.

...WE KEEP BUYING THEM.

WE'RE PUPPETS OF THE FASHION WORLD, EL. IF THEY TELL US IT LOOKS GOOD ON US, WE RUSH OUT AND BUY IT!

the SUMMER SHOPPE

...IT'S LIKE THE EMPEROR'S NEW CLOTHES!

The Summer Sho

BATHING SU SALE

BUT THE EMPEROR WASN'T WEARING ANYTHING!!

EXACTLY.

SALE

WHAT'S THE MATTER, EL?

CONNIE AND I WENT SHOPPING FOR BATHING SUITS.

I'M TELLING YOU, ANNE - THERE'S NOTHING OUT THERE TO FLATTER THE TWO-BABY FIGURE!!

WHAT HAPPENED TO THE CUPS? THE RUFFLES? THE SKIRTS AND IN- SERTS? WHAT HAPPENED TO THE SUITS THAT CAMOUFLAGED INSTEAD OF LETTING IT ALL HANG OUT?!!

I DUNNO...MAYBE IT WAS THE NEW LAWS THAT GOVERN TRUTH IN ADVERTISING.

WHO WAS ON THE PHONE, EL?

ED. THELMA BAIRD'S FRIEND.

REALLY? HOW IS THE OLD DOLL?

JOHN.... SHE DIED LAST NIGHT.

MRS. BAIRD? SHE'S DEAD? BUT HOW? WHY?

WELL, SHE WAS IN HER 80S, ELIZABETH, AND I GUESS SHE HAD A STROKE LAST NIGHT, AND....

IT'S OK, HONEY. IT HAPPENED SO FAST. IT WAS QUICK AND EASY FOR HER.

BUT IT'S NOT EASY FOR THE REST OF US!

I WENT DOWN TO THE LODGE TO SEE ED. HE'S VERY UPSET, BUT HE SAYS HE'LL BE ALL RIGHT.

LOOK. THELMA ASKED HIM TO GIVE ME THIS CEDAR CHEST BEFORE SHE DIED. SHE BOUGHT IT IN CHINA YEARS AGO.

BUT IT'S EMPTY!

NO, IT ISN'T, MIKE. THIS CHEST IS FULL OF MEMORIES.

111

I CAN'T SLEEP, ELIZABETH .... I'VE NEVER KNOWN ANYBODY WHO'S DIED BEFORE.

ME NEITHER.

MRS. BAIRD WAS SUCH A NICE LADY. I CAN'T BELIEVE SHE'S GONE.

DON'T CRY, MICHAEL.

.... NOW WE KNOW OUR VERY OWN ANGEL!

YES, OK, TWO BOUQUETS WILL BE NICE. HOW MANY PEOPLE? THEN WE'LL NEED THE CORNER LOUNGE.

SANDWICHES, TEA, COFFEE—WHAT ABOUT SOFT DRINKS?

EVERYONE'S GOING TO SO MUCH TROUBLE TO ORGANIZE THELMA'S FUNERAL....

..... WHY DIDN'T WE DO SOMETHING FOR HER WHILE SHE WAS ALIVE?!

SHE WAS THE LIGHT OF MY LIFE THESE PAST FEW MONTHS, ELLY. THEL AND I EVEN TALKED ABOUT MARRIAGE.

I KNOW.

I'M REALLY GOING TO MISS HER. BUT PERHAPS I'LL SEE HER AGAIN BEFORE TOO LONG.

DON'T LOOK AT ME LIKE THAT. I'M 86, AND NOBODY LIVES FOREVER!

AND WHEN I SEE HER, I'LL GIVE HER A HUG FROM YOU.

BE QUIET, LIZZIE... REALLY QUIET.

SEE THEM? SEE THE BABY BIRDS? THERE'S FOUR OF THEM!

FOUR BRAND-NEW BABIES IN THE WORLD!

IT'S MAGIC, ISN'T IT!

WHAT'S UP THERE?

A NEST WITH FOUR NEW BABY BIRDS.

IT'S A NICE NEST, MICHAEL, AN' IT'S ALL LINED WITH DOWN PLUCKED FROM THE MOTHER!

WATCH. THE BIG BIRDS GO BACK AN' FORTH ALL DAY GETTING BUGS AN' STUFF!

....IT'S NICE TO KNOW WE'RE NOT THE ONLY PARENTS WHO SACRIFICE FOR THEIR CHILDREN.

I'M GOING TO DRIVE OLD ED OUT TO THE CEMETERY, JOHN. I'LL BE BACK SOON!

HEY, MOM - GOING DOWNTOWN? COULD YOU PICK UP SOME VIDEOS?

I WANT PIZZA! COULD YOU GET SOME PIZZA?

ONE LIFE STOPS.... BUT THE REST GO ON

SORT OF A PEACEFUL SPOT. ISN'T IT.

THELMA WANTED TO BE BURIED NEXT TO HER HUSBAND. ...DEAR GOD, I MISS HER.

SOME DAY— I'LL BE OVER THERE NEXT TO MY WIFE.

I NEVER HAD A COMPLICATED LOVE LIFE IN THIS WORLD. I HOPE THE FOUR OF US CAN SORT THINGS OUT IN THE NEXT ONE.

Lynn

GOODBYE, ED. I'LL SEE YOU ON THE WEEKEND. COME FOR SUPPER!

THAT WILL BE NICE.

YOU KNOW, THE LODGE IS A NICE PLACE TO LIVE... BUT THERE'S NOTHING LIKE GOOD HOME COOKING!!

WELL, MY COOKING MIGHT NOT BE THE BEST IN THE WORLD!

THAT'S OK! I'M COMING FOR THE HOME PART!!

Lynn

NA, NA, NA-NAAAH-NA! CAN'T CATCH ME!

I DON'T WANT TO CATCH YOU

WART HEAD! WART HEAD! CAN'T CATCH ME!

I DON'T HAVE THE SLIGHTEST DESIRE TO CATCH YOU, ELIZABETH.

STICK YER TOES UP YER NOSE, CAN'T CATCH.....

GOTCHA!!!

Lynn

DARNED STOVE! THIS THING DRIVES ME CRAZY — AND THIS DRAWER WON'T WORK!

LOOK OUT, FARLEY! THERE'S NOT ENOUGH ROOM FOR THE TWO OF US IN HERE!!

HAVING TROUBLE WITH SUPPER, HONEY? IS THERE ANYTHING I CAN DO TO HELP?

YES!

REMODEL THE KITCHEN!!

REMODEL THE KITCHEN? BUT....

IT'S OVER 18 YEARS OLD, JOHN! THE APPLIANCES ARE ANTIQUES, THE CUPBOARDS ARE WARPED, THE LINOLEUM NEEDS REPLACING....

LOOK AT THE TOASTER! IT'S HELD TOGETHER BY MASKING TAPE AND 6 YEARS' WORTH OF BREAD CRUMBS! I NEED SOME CHANGES HERE!

RIGHT.

WE'LL GET A NEW TOASTER!!

ELLY WANTS TO REMODEL THE KITCHEN, JEAN... WHY WOULD SHE WANT TO DO THAT?

SURE, PUT A LITTLE PAINT ON, BUY A NEW STOVE, BUT REMODELING COSTS A FORTUNE!

OH, COME ON WITH THE EXPENSE BIT. SHE SAID YOU NEVER EVEN FLINCHED WHEN YOU PAID FOR THAT SPORTS CAR LAST FALL!

SOMETHING TELLS ME I'M GOING TO PAY FOR THAT SPORTS CAR FOR THE REST OF MY LIFE.

NOPE, YOU'RE WRONG ABOUT REMODELING, DOC. ELLY DESERVES A NEW KITCHEN.

AUTOCLAVE

WHERE ARE YOU GOING?

TO FIND TED AND SEE HOW HE FEELS ABOUT IT.

BUT TED IS THE BIGGEST BUTT OF MALE CHAUVINIST PORKDOM IN THE BUILDING!

I KNOW.

I WANT TO TALK TO SOMEONE WHO'LL AGREE WITH ME.

Lynn

HI, HONEY!... ER, WHAT'S THIS?

BLACKENED MEATLOAF.

OH.

IS THAT SOMETHING YOU MAKE WITH CAJUN SPICES?

NO.

IT'S SOMETHING YOU MAKE WHEN YOUR OVEN WORKS ONLY ON "BROIL."

Lynn

OK...THE WAY YOU'D LIKE TO DO IT, EL....I FIGURE IT'LL COST $10,000 TO REMODEL THIS KITCHEN

—UNLESS, OF COURSE, I DO IT MYSELF!

BUT, UH, WOULDN'T IT BE BETTER IF WE HIRED A PROFESSIONAL?

HONEY, I'M A DENTIST! I AM A PROFESSIONAL!

JOHN, IF YOU'RE GOING TO REBUILD THE KITCHEN, SHOULDN'T YOU DRAW UP SOME PLANS? MEASURE THE COUNTERS, CUPBOARDS, THINGS LIKE THAT?

SAY, GREG—DO YOU HAVE A GOOD 16-FOOT TAPE?

SURE!

GOT SOME BIG PROJECT IN MIND?

YOU MIGHT SAY THAT.

THE WIFE WANTS ME TO TAKE HER MEASUREMENTS.

THIS IS OUR "COUNTRY CLASSIC" WITH WALNUT FINISH AND PORCELAIN PULLS...

AND THIS IS WHAT WE CALL OUR "HEIRLOOM!"

WHAT DO YOU THINK, JOHN?

LET'S GO WITH THE "HEIRLOOM".

JUDGING FROM WHAT THIS IS GOING TO COST.... THE KIDS MIGHT INHERIT THE PAYMENTS!

DO YOU WANT TO DO A 3-PIN AMALGAM ON MRS. MADDEN'S M.O.D. - OR PREPARE IT FOR A CROWN?

UH?

DR. PATTERSON, YOU ARE OBSESSED WITH RE-MODELLING THAT KITCHEN!

I'M NOT OBSESSED, JEAN. WHEN I'M AT WORK, I FORGET EVERYTHING BUT THE PATIENT.

.... PASS ME THE LINOLEUM.

WHAT'S GOING ON? ARE WE MOVING?

I'M CLEANING OUT THE KITCHEN SO DADDY CAN TEAR OUT THE CUPBOARDS!

WHERE WILL WE EAT?

I'VE GOT A HOTPLATE IN THE BASEMENT.

DON'T WORRY, GUYS! DADDY KNOWS WHAT HE'S DOING!

120

HEY! THAT'S A GOOD COUNTERTOP THERE, JOHN! DO YOU WANT IT?

NO - IT'D PROBABLY JUST SIT IN MY GARAGE FOR 10 YEARS 'TIL I THREW IT OUT!

WHAT'S HE GONNA DO WITH IT?

....LET IT SIT IN HIS GARAGE FOR 10 YEARS 'TIL HE THROWS IT OUT!

I'M GLAD YOU'RE GETTING A NEW KITCHEN, EL - BUT YOUR RENOVATIONS ARE DRIVING ME CRAZY!

WHY?

EVERY TIME JOHN BRINGS OUT AN OLD SINK OR A CUPBOARD DOOR, HE GIVES IT TO STEVE, AND STEVE PILES IT HERE.

DOESN'T HE HAVE PLANS FOR THEM?

SURE. HE HAS PLANS FOR ALL THIS STUFF.

BUT, HE NEVER DOES ANY-THING WITH IT!!!

I MARRIED A PACK RAT, EL. LOOK IN MY BASEMENT, UNDER THE PORCH - THERE'S EVERYTHING FROM CLOCK PARTS TO SHEET METAL!

THIS ISN'T A HOUSE.... IT'S A SCRAPYARD!!

I WANT SOME SPACE!! I WANT TO GET RID OF THIS STUFF! I WANT TO CALL SOMEONE AND HAVE IT HAULED AWAY!

WELL.... WHY DON'T YOU?!

BECAUSE I WANT HIM, TOO.

DON'T THROW OUT THAT POTATO SALAD, JOHN—IT'S STILL GOOD!

BUT NOBODY WANTS IT—

I'LL EAT IT, THEN.

WHY? THERE'S NOTHING WRONG WITH THROWING OUT A LITTLE FOOD.

HOW CAN YOU SAY THAT WITH PEOPLE HUNGRY ALL OVER THE WORLD?!!

.... I'M EATING FOR MILLIONS.

I CAN'T HELP IT, ANNIE.. I WAS TAUGHT TO EAT EVERYTHING ON MY PLATE—I CAN'T STAND THROWING FOOD AWAY!

IF THERE'S FOOD LEFT IN THE POT, I EAT IT. IF THE KIDS DON'T FINISH, I EAT IT—I CANNOT WASTE A THING!!

SO FEED IT TO THE DOG!

ARE YOU CRAZY? YOU WANT HIM TO GET FAT ?!!

LOOK, EL...IF YOU HATE TO WASTE FOOD, ALL YOU HAVE TO DO IS FOLLOW THE THREE C'S.

ONE: "COMPANY" INVITE SOMEONE OVER. TWO: "COMPOST" RECYCLE VEGGIE SCRAPS AS FERTILIZER...

AND THREE?

CASSEROLE!

TRUST ME, STEVE...IT NEVER PAYS TO LISTEN IN TO FEMALE CONVERSATION

WHERE ARE YOU TWO GOING?
INTO THE HOUSE.

WELL, THERE'S A LOT OF CONSTRUCTION GOING ON IN THERE.. I DON'T WANT YOU GETTING INTO ANY TROUBLE.

CHEEZ!! SHE TREATS ME LIKE A BABY! WHAT KINDA TROUBLE COULD WE GET INTO IN HERE ANYHOW?!

I DUNNO...BUT MAYBE WE CAN FIND SOMETHING!!

HOW LONG DO YOU GUYS HAFTA EAT IN THE BASEMENT?
'TILL THE KITCHEN'S FINISHED

WE BORROWED A CAMP STOVE, AN' A MINI FRIDGE AN...
HEY! YOU GOT A MICROWAVE!!

FAR OUT, MAN! EVER PUT A FLY IN ONE OF THEM THINGS? POW!! THEY LAST ABOUT 30 SECONDS!!

GORDON, THAT'S GROSS!
YEAH!! WANNA TRY IT?

WATCHA LOOKIN' FOR?
BUGS!

GORDON WANTS TO PUT A BUG IN THE MICROWAVE, LIZZIE— WANNA WATCH?

OH, WOW! A SPIDER!! CHECK THE SIZE OF IT, MAN! THIS SUCKER'LL GO UP LIKE A ROCKET!!

SAY YOUR PRAYERS, SPIDER....YOU'RE GONNA FRY!!

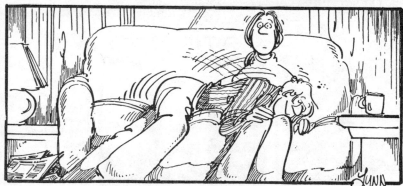

HE'S CRAWLIN' AROUND!

OK, MAN... SET 'ER FOR 30 SECONDS. READY... AIM......

HI, GUYS! WHAT ARE YOU SO BUSY WITH?

UH? NOTHIN'!!!

SOMETHING WRONG WITH THE MICRO-WAVE, GORDON?

UH... NO! WHY?!!

GOOD – I THOUGHT YOU MIGHT LIKE TO STAY FOR DINNER!

WAIT!!! DON'T TURN ON THAT OVEN!!!

WHY NOT?

THERE'S A SPIDER IN THERE! MIKE AN' GORDON WERE GONNA NUKE IT!!

IT WAS JUST AN EX-PERIMENT – HONEST! WE DIDN'T MEAN ANY HARM!

TELL THAT TO THE SPIDER!!!

OK, WE GOT THE SPIDER OUT OF THE MICROWAVE. WHERE DO YOU WANT US TO PUT IT?

OUTSIDE.

WHAT YOU WERE ABOUT TO DO WAS CRUEL AND HORRIBLE! HE HAS AS MUCH RIGHT TO LIVE AS YOU DO! .....SET HIM FREE!!

"CHOMP"!!

WHAT'S THAT? THEY DELIVERED THE FRIDGE TODAY.

WHY DIDN'T THEY PUT IT INSIDE? I DON'T KNOW! I WASN'T HERE. THEY WERE SUPPOSED TO COME TOMORROW!

WHAT?! THEY'VE LEFT ME TO CARRY A 2,000-LB. FRIDGE UP THOSE STAIRS?!!

IT'S OK, DADDY! ... I'LL HELP!

ARRGHHHH! NNNHHHGGG!! HRMMPH!!!

WELL, IT SURE WAS NICE OF YOU TWO TO HELP US MOVE THAT FRIDGE! SURE! NO PROBLEM! ANY TIME!

DO ME A FAVOR, CONNIE ....THE NEXT TIME THE PATTERSONS CALL UP AND SAY, "ARE YOU GUYS BUSY TONIGHT?"...... ASK WHY!!

NEXT WEEK? OH. ...BUT YOU SAID YOU'D INSTALL THEM TWO WEEKS AGO!

YES, I KNOW YOU'RE BUSY. YES, I CAN SYMPATHIZE. REALLY. WELL, I DON'T MEAN TO BE A NUISANCE. SURE I CAN WAIT. NEXT WEEK WILL BE FINE.

WHAT'S A MATTER, MOM? WHY AREN'T OUR NEW CUPBOARDS READY?

... I'M TOO NICE.